My Window Prayer

Catherine Florel

WestBow
PRESS
A DIVISION OF THOMAS NELSON

Copyright © 2013 Catherine Florel.

All rights reserved. No part of this book may be used or reproduced by any means, graphic, electronic, or mechanical, including photocopying, recording, taping or by any information storage retrieval system without the written permission of the publisher except in the case of brief quotations embodied in critical articles and reviews.

WestBow Press books may be ordered through booksellers or by contacting:

WestBow Press
A Division of Thomas Nelson
1663 Liberty Drive
Bloomington, IN 47403
www.westbowpress.com
1-(866) 928-1240

Because of the dynamic nature of the Internet, any web addresses or links contained in this book may have changed since publication and may no longer be valid. The views expressed in this work are solely those of the author and do not necessarily reflect the views of the publisher, and the publisher hereby disclaims any responsibility for them.

Any people depicted in stock imagery provided by Thinkstock are models, and such images are being used for illustrative purposes only.

Certain stock imagery © Thinkstock.

ISBN: 978-1-4497-8259-7 (sc)
ISBN: 978-1-4497-8258-0 (e)

Library of Congress Control Number: 2013901236

Printed in the United States of America

WestBow Press rev. date: 2/6/2013

Dedicated to my husband, children and grandchildren,
May they always know I love them.

Part One

Some how the Supreme Court has decided that life does not start in the womb. Well I am here to tell you it does. I am living proof of how the rejection of ones parent in the womb can cause a person to have no worth or value. When that first value of love is deynied the emotional growth stops also. My story starts there in the womb with one parent not giving love all through his life and death.

There was thirty-three years difference in the ages of my parents and my jealous father could not bring himself to believe his young wife was pergnant with his child. So I was not held or hugged or kissed or loved by my father. I never got to sit on his lap. Never was appreciated or had my existance aknowleged. How can a person take such an extreme punishment out on a child? How can mankind be so cruel?

The story of my rejection does not end there. My mother was not a person with the warmth of hugs and kisses either. She was always trying to better me or should I say make me a lady. I didn't talk right, walk right, laugh right, and was to fat. Such helpful advice was perceived as not being good enough. Words can hurt even if they are meant in good faith that they will better that person.

My Window Prayer

There also was violence in my home. After a night of drinking there was a round of wife beating. My brother and I would be woken up to come rescue our mother. Many times we were to hide out until morning.

My brother was three years older and not much better off than I was accept he was the male child and was acceptable to our father. We were not close even with only the two of us. We were not taught by word or example to love each other.

We were raised in a rural area and there were only boys to play with so my brother had friends. There weren't any girls. So I lived in my imagination. The cousins were boys also and not much for a girl to learn how to get on with girls. My nickname was crybaby. I was the youngest and picked on.

The school was not much better for a girl without any social skills. I was a loner all the way through. There were very few dates and no prom. If I had lived in this time I wonder if I would have been teased and tortured like those of today. I did have some bullying, but very little. Not like the ones today.

Well the story goes on and I did marry and have children. Five in seven and a half years. With no coping skills and a run down body I found myself in a depression and was thinking about how I wanted out. I went to visit with a friend and was very sad and was relating to her my tale of woe. My friend didn't know what to say to my depressed state. She shook her head and said that she took her things to God. So I found myself at my bedroom window saying: God, if there is a God at all, where in the h★★★ are you.

Part Two

There was no fan fare, high emotional state or any noticeable change in me at the time. I can tell you in hindsight that the Holy Spirit came to me that day. There were quiet little changes that happened. One of the first memories I have is the bookmobile stopping on our corner that summer. Never happened before or since and I went and got a book. That was something I didn't do because I was a poor reader. As a matter of fact I can only remember reading one other book. The book was a love story and I can remember thinking what was love. That word stuck out in my mind.

The next thing I remember was a person giving me a present, the only one she ever gave me before or after, for my birthday. The book was "Satan is Alive and Well on Earth " by Hal Lindsey. By this time my mother had led me into the occult and this was an awakening. My mother had stored some things in my basement. I had a dream about snakes in my basement and I knew I had to clean out all the stuff my mother had brought into my home from the occult. Than I went around with holy water and prayed.

Another little thing that happened that made a big difference in my growth was a friend was having a little bible study before lent in women's group and I was encouraged to come. So I did. The stories we were assigned to read in the bible came alive. There was a woman there that was experiencing the same thing. We were just so excited and by the end of six weeks the others were in tears because they were not getting the same thing out of the stories. This other woman was after me to come with her to a meeting. Having read about Satan and occult I was very leery of it all. But she convinced me to attend. That was the start of real growth. These were baby steps and now the work really began.

The meeting was done in an informal way with the lady in charged having become a Spiritual Director because of her own way to God. It was like listening to Greek for me, a hole new world. The instructions were very simple. Get on your knees morning, noon, and night. Ask God to give you the meekness and humility of Jesus Christ, and to take my will and give his will in return. At night was to go over your day and confess your sins and ask for the opposite virtue.

Well it did start to make since to me and led me to the laments. There is nine of them starting with God Where Are You. These were given to my as I sat at my dining room table. I just kept writing and feeling.

God Where Are You

Help! Help! The Pain! Where am I! Who am I!

I am held captive by the Prince of darkness, the mind bender, the creator of selfishness and deceit. I sit here in darkness of sin, blinded by the spiral cylinder created by self-love. It has enveloped me, case me into a prison bound with chains that have been formed by links of pride, covetousness, sloth, lust, gluttony, envy, anger, and their children.

My heart is starting to cry. I feel the pain and hunger of a no deposit, no return love life I have lived. The word charity haunts me. That word: To give to and for someone else. Oh what a word.

Catherine Florel

Where is my friend? Where is the One who holds the key? Where is the One that has been chained for me? He cries to me and I am bound. He asks of me and I do not know why I can not move. I am bound and in prison. There I am, on a tread mill exhausted from the search. What can I do to feel the presence the heart wants to touch? Touch me, please touch me, please touch me.

I feel the cold body. The cold and lonely body that has been captured by the sin. The body that houses the nothing of selfishness. It can not stand the idea of self imposed pain. How can a life that has not wanted anything but love have pushed away, run, hidden, and demanded sin to stand for so long.

Now I know who I am. A sinner. A lonely, crying out sinner. My heart is broken my mind is out of order, my body is beaten, my soul is longing for the inhabitation of the Holy Spirit.

Come Lord of love, Lord of charity, Lord of salvation, Lord JESUS CHRIST. I invite You into my heart, my soul, and my mind, to be with me 'til the end of time.

Praise be the name of the Lord Jesus. Praise to the God who has created love. My friend, I am lonely for You.

Teach me to be!

Coming from a background of Saturday religion classed I didn't retain much of anything about God and Jesus. I know the answer to why are we here. We are here to know love and service God. What that meant was a mystery to me.

My Window Prayer

One of the things I can tell you is the Holy Spirit helps you to know your sins. I was getting to know that I had to stop looking at other people and start looking at me. I could blame my parents, but I found that they had their skeletons in their closets too. Their childhood's left a lot to be desired. They could have written their own books. When Jesus says forgive them they don't know what they do, it can apply to all of us. The fact that they were not responsible for my miserable childhood was something that I had a hard time with. But by the grace of God there go I. So, taking responsibility for my self has been a life long process. The pain was coming from not knowing how to handle it and not knowing that all things were to go back to God. I needed healing from God. Turning all this over to God was the only way I could stop the blame.

I found that God was in my life all along. One time that was very clear was the time that he gave me a miracle. After having a 54-hr. labor with my first child, I was 36-hrs.into labor with my second child. I was about 41/2 to 5 dilations and I said the Our Father because I had read that someone had done that. The nurse had her hand on my stomach and she said your stomach popped. Just like that I was wheeled into the delivery room. My baby was born with short order. That was before my window prayer. That still didn't bring to me the realization that God did exist, but he was there.

The time I almost drowned and God was there to make sure I survived. Again this was before my prayer. I was almost compromised by a neighbor boy but my mother came out in time. There were times I could go back and see Gods footprints.

Learning whom God is has taken a lifetime. I know I will be finished only when I am lucky enough to warrant heaven at the end of my time here. God is Love and it is I who has to learn the unconditionally way of loving. The one thing I do know is that God doesn't think like I do and has different reasons for the things that happen. Also he can not cross the will of others. He gave us all free will and he does not cross it. This is one of the hardest thoughts to get through. He doesn't cross the will of anybody. Even the will of the people who killed Jesus was not crossed.

Alone   2

Alone, so empty and alone.

I am so alone Lord. I can't stand it. The tears are streaming down my checks. Where is my friend? Where are the people? How can I find the peace? My heart is shattered in a million pieces. I have given the children back their lives. My husband has his life back and he running away from me. He can't stand to hear me. My friends are not hearing me they don't look for me.

That song, "What a friend we have in Jesus" is driving me nuts. Where are You? Where is the peace? What world am I in? I know the truth of this out of control society we live in. When I speak of it, I know I'm not part of it. All I feel is loneliness. Oh how it hurts.

Catherine Florel

The pain is coming from expectations. I want my family to love me. I want my world to revolve around me. I can not have it my way. To love is hard. To love and be without sin is hard. No, to love in spite of sin is what You are calling me to do. Oh that's big. In spite of what is in my day I must be unselfish enough to love. No matter how I am threatened or no mater what is said. You want me to leave the sinner to You and clean up my life.

That judge in me is not happy. You are the judge of sin and most of all, the sinner. I must not allow my sin to come up against another but act in love. An apostle is to feed the lambs. Feed them with love. Perfect love. A love that won't leave them lonely. A Christ like person feeding love. A love for another's gain, the gain of heaven.

Oh Lord, me an Apostle. You sure have Your work cut out for You. I am the captain judge of my world. I guess to be honest the whole world. To love another unselfishly, is to love no matter what and leave the sinner in Your Hands.

But Lord what about the emptiness I am crying from? If I get out of the way long enough, I won't be lonely. If I use the love You give for that day there will be more tomorrow. Please Lord I need to get out of the way again. If self could die just a little each day love could grow a little each day.

Fill me. FILL ME WITH LOVE, PLEASE LORD JUSUS.

I know there is where I will find You.

One of the things I could say here is that "no one can make you happy." Part of that is true, but you can be happy and have a good time with others. The hard part is to learn that expectations have to die. Judgement has to die. To let other people be who they are and except them there is the path. However, it takes God himself to accomplish this.

You can be alone in a crowd. That was where I lived. Now I can be in my home and not be lonely. Loneliness is from a need in us. When we don't get that first value of love, we just keep looking for it. It takes the healing of God to be no longer alone.

Do I enjoy company, you bet. The difference is I don't need them. There is still a part of me that wants my brother to love me, to care about my life. He is also looking for that first love and is rapped up in telling me all about his life. Like I said it takes time to learn to love. We always think that our family should know how to love us and care about us. Most of us come from a place where the world revolves around us. We are the center and what we think is the way it is. The fact is that we are all looking for someone to see us and love us.

My expectation of having a friend that would go shopping and do things with has not come to pass, but I do have to true friend that knows me warts and all. Concepts are hard to brake and the one I had about a friend was hard to brake. The bible says, "If you have one true friend you are blessed". I am blessed.

When you are looking for love and friendship, you are not alone. People want you to listen and care about them. I am learning to listen and respond with the support that is needed. There is the key to a real friendship. It should be a two way street, someone that is willing to listen to you. There was a time when my responses were not there. I was numb and unresponsive not knowing what to do, or thinking what I was going to say. There is much to learn about being with people. It is hard to listen to just listen, but that is what is the best way for me to learn to be present to someone else.

Am I Threatened 3

Lord God, creator of love, hope, faith, and my desire for the truth. You are threatening to me. What a threat. What a treat to let go. Help me! Help me! Your son is here and knocking on my door. Open up. Open up. Open up my heart. Oh the treat.

To leave my life in Your hands. To give the control over to You. To give in love is to let go of all, yes all controls on my family and me. Now that I have learned to control my life you ask me to give it up. To give until I die. To leave the result in Your hands and not to expect the results I desire.

To act on the knowledge that You are there with everything under Your control. Acting on unseen, unfelt, and ununderstood action is so foreign to me. To know You are there and Your faithfulness is everlasting. To bring that hope into my life. Oh that threatens me.

I must believe to the degree of death. To know I do not, but You must have my life and the lives of my family. Like Abraham, I must bring to the altar the living, the dead, the sick, the very ones my life revolves around, and me and walk away. And walk away. Leave. Let go.

I must trust. I must TRUST. I know You will show me what I must know. I know I can trust You, but I know I can't let go. I want to know what is going on. Please Lord Jesus, walk in front of me. Keep me in my place. Help me to trust in faith, love, and hope. It is I who stops the work that the Father does in me.

God loves in perfect form. He loves me and mine in perfect form. Not as I love but as I should love with no strings. Love with complete charity for me. Did I say for me? Yes for ME! Oh Lord how can that threaten me.

Love, what a power.

Now we are talking TRUST! I can tell you if you had a childhood like mine the last thing you can do is trust. The very idea that there is someone with my best interest is nonexistent. The battle of now giving trust to someone you can not see is hard. By this time I knew enough to believe there is someone directing me, but how do I trust?

It's one thing to say a prayer and give up the things to

God. To picture it all in a bag and leave it at the altar, it's another thing to leave it there. Hundreds of times I would start thinking about the problem and have to again and again try to give it up. It was a battle. Knowing all things work for good with God was not helping to leave it in God's hands.

When time and again things did not go my way I would question the wisdom. I did not see this as the growth I needed to trust. I did not see that all things in their time. That required patience and I was short on that also. The mind of God is not like mine and I will always be thinking in my box and He the whole instead of just the present. My thinking had to change. My expectations, needs, concepts, and ideas were just that mine. Did that change? Yes, and did that bring peace, yes. Sometimes I slip and have to learn to accept as things are.

There are some things that you can change and some things that you have to except. Knowing the difference is hard. Some times the Lord had to bring me up very hard to get my attention. His voice is quiet and I am not, so it was hard not to get into trouble before it became clear what was to be done. Thank God, He never gives up on me, even when my faith becomes that of a mustard seed.

Giving back the good things in our life is also hard. But hanging on to them leads to pride, as if I had something to do with the good, but not the bad. Not giving up the good stops the growth again. I know that I can only be humble if I except the good was from God and it had to go back.

If I don't let go, I get in the way. I can tie God's hands if I get into the way. God's love if perfect and mine is not. Which way would I have it, that is a no brainer. Trust is the biggest thing for me to do. The feeling sometimes is that things will not go my way is getting in the way. There have been times that I learn later that things work out different than I thought, but the results are better in the end. One of the things that are hard to believe is that my feelings lie to me. Feelings cannot be trusted. So in all things give to God.

Enemies

Why is there war in my house? Why are we all at war? What happened to love?

When did the parents become the enemy? When did I lose the friendly closeness?

When Jesus went to the temple for the first time and He went about His Father's business why did He bring Mary up so short? How much privacy do we give our children? How come my husband sees me as an Enemy? I can't stand being the guard. I hate being the one who has all the dirty work. Help me to see where love went. Help me to bring peace to my house.

Mary seemed to know what it was her son was saying. Was it time to not police or was it time to let the Father take over or was it time to let them fall. Oh Lord I can hardly write that. To fall. To hit rock bottom. To hit rock bottom in this world today can be------ I can't even find the words. My kids face today things that are far more damaging to them than was ever known when I was young.

The miracles will be greater in that day then I have performed. Isn't that what You said? There is a greater need for greater miracles today than yesterday and it is getting worse at a faster rate. I forgot Your promise again. Do not worry. But what about my responsibility? I can't leave them go and run or can I. Do I set the rules and not follow through?

Mary knew something I can't get my finger on. Worry seems to be the key. Do not worry in that day what you will say. Do what you can and let the rest go. Let go. Don't worry. I am there.

Your are here! YOU ARE HERE! Your are my eyes, my mouth, my mind, my protector and my advisor. You told me my children are saved. You told me.

Relax, let go, let God. But there is war.

Make peace. How?

Teach them to love. Teach them to let go. Teach them to love.

Teach by example.

Oh Lord that takes real strength and courage. More courage than I have ever had before.

My Window Prayer

Fill me with the power of Your love. My love is not strong enough.

Worrying seemed to be my lives work. I didn't know what I was doing. I was about thirty or thirty-one when I prayed at my window. Nothing happens over night and this did require work. Knowing nothing about how a happy orderly home was run, it did have to be God's work if this was going to change.

One of the things that were happening in the house was the not so nice, the comments the kids were making to each other. They were getting an allowance and when I would hear one of those comments I would deduct some of the allowance. At the end of the week every one got a different amount of money. The backbiting got better every week until I could once again give them all of their money. This brought some of that peace I so longed for. It also showed me that God was there, helping me to clean the mess I made with my lack of knowledge.

The power struggles with the kids were being handled with little or no resistance because of the absence of sin, my sin, of anger, demanding, and not listening. I learned to making my answers once and final unless there was more information coming or the attitude of the child improved. I didn't speak to attitude. God gave me the strong back to face the need to fallow through. To not demand but expect obedience. They could trust what I said because I was consistent with my discipline. We had our moments but with God's grace we got through them. Peace was slow but it came.

Communication is very important to the peace in a home. So much of the war can be misunderstanding. But there are degrees of love and giving in a family and it does take a willingness to better ourselves. To work to the end of war and make peace.

I found myself between the kids and their father. They came to me, and he came to me. I was the bad guy for him. Well, I gave back his responsibility for his relationship with his kids to him. What a burden off my shoulders. The tiger was more of a pussycat without the buffer. Again there was more peace in the house. It is nice to see the family together and enjoying each other. I learned relationships have to some extent be between the two people involved unless there is violence or dominance.

Things in a home go better when the parents are on the same page. The kids pick up on the division and use it to pit the parents against each other. Learning to work things out with maturity, away from the children. There is an art to arguing to come to a working relationship. Again the parties should try to be willing to come to an agreement if possible. Some people will not give, or refuse to see the whole picture. God is always my answer. If you want peace make peace.

Marriage

Oh Lord how I long for a happy marriage!

What do I do with a mate that doesn't know how to love me or the children? What do I do with the responsibility of two? What do I do with his out of God's order responses? My heart aches with sorrow over what should be.

A machine can't function when one-half isn't working, what about a marriage? My heart cries for the children. My loneliness sometimes comes up and strangles me. Sometimes I think it would be easier not knowing God's beautiful plan for a man and his wife.

The Bible says to be submissive and husband loves your wife. It says, "obey your husbands, so that any of them who do not believe in the Word of the gospel may be won over apart from preaching, through their wives' conduct." Lord how this makes me cry.

I must protect the children. I can't let him steal his love or mine from the children. Is that my guideline Lord? Loving the children. They are God given. Love the children. Again You ask me to die to myself and love. God blessed me with children. They are my husband's also and he is blessed. You love us both. You brought me faith through the children.

Without my children I can do anything I want. I could become as selfish as I wanted or as spoiled as I wanted, and I would never know the real world of God. The real world.

God loves my children. They are blessings given to purify my love AND my husband's. I have learned more about love through my children than I have or could through my husband.

Marriage is God's house for his children. Marriage is the foundation for creation. Creating people, Christian people and a Christian world. Two people creating a church. Wherever two or more are gathered in MY NAME. In God. Under God. In obedience.

You love my husband and his children. I will protect the children as best I can and leave his conversion in Your hands. I know now that You want those kids to have two parents, and You will be there with me as their Father and with me as I am willing to be willing to love them. Because You love the children You will keep the grace flowing to their father.

My Window Prayer

Help me to stay out of Your way. Help me to act on Your word. Marriage is sacred.

My husband and I have not had a childhood that taught us about marriage. There wasn't any model to go by. Marriage takes two people working at it 100%. The Bible tells you what love is suppose to look like. Love is patient, love is kind, and so on. When you go to a wedding many times this passage is read. What is not read is how do you put this into practice. It is said that women are from Venus and men are from Mars. What I found is we don't think alike. Communication is one very important issue. What did I say that has you up in arms? How can two people who come from different backgrounds come gather?

How do you treat one another? Are you selfish? Does everything have to be your way? Do you compromise? Do you nag? Do you tell another what is wrong with them and not see yourself? Do you go out once and awhile and just have fun? Do you have fun? Are you always looking at the glass half empty or half full? Do you take care of the things that are your duty to the family? Do you use your manners? Do you appreciate all the little things or big things that your partner does? Do you thank them for just doing their job? Do you talk nice to them as you do to your friends? Are you giving your 100% or are you looking for their 100%?

Intimacy is not sexual in a marriage. It is getting to

know someone in an intimate way. Being there to be to a support, or knowing the likes and dislikes. Being trustworthy enough to share the most intimate times. To open up and let it all out. Only reacting in love and understanding can bring this to pass. To keep secret the things that are not for others to know. I think trust is the number one stumbling block for intimacy. Do you trust the one you live with?

Can we achieve this? We can only keep working on marriage. Keeping in mind that we also have to give that person to God. Let go and let that person be who they are. We are not our mate's keepers. They have to come to this and so do you, but on our own. You can not make anyone into a good mate, only make your own marriage what it is in your power to do.

There is so much divorce in this world today. Why? We are looking for that first value of love in our mates. They can not give that to you. Only God can heel you. And healing is what is needed in all of us. My reward is in heaven and I can only try to get there by doing what I can to give my 100%. Sometimes it may be 90 or even 50 but I keep trying.

The way of love is in knowledge. Feelings can lie to you. Romance can be a start, but deep mature love takes time and work. Chose to love in all things. Chose to love in spite of your feelings. Recognizing the way each gives to the other in ways of love. There is a book about 5 different ways to love that teaches there are many ways to show love. To be willing to be willing to learn and grow hopefully with both working toward this.

There are situations that require help. It is wise to seek help to do what can be done to for the continuation of the marriage. Of course if there is danger help must be sought immediately.

Games

Oh the games people play! I am manipulated. I am naïve!

Oh Lord how it hurts. Why am I the one who seems to always get the shaft? I trust the ones who are supposed to love me. I seem to be coming up short or on the short end. Why am I always the last to know? Somehow I end up doing the very thing I didn't want to do.

I am a giving person by nature. Although I have on occasion been sneaky, I do not try and manipulate, or am I fooling myself? Do we and are we all playing games to get what we want from others. Oh Lord once again I feel tricked and once again I feel that I have been sitting with my head in the sand.

Catherine Florel

I am not dumb or am I stupid. My mind is very quick. Naïve is the word. Naïve: having or showing natural simplicity of nature; 1. unsophisticated; ingenuous. 2. Having or showing a lack of experience, judgment or information. Ingenuous: 1. Characterized by cleverness or originality of invention or construction. 2. Cleverly inventive; resourceful. Isn't everyone!

All my life I have been naïve. The people in my life have always been able to get what they wanted from me. Never did I hide anything from them. Just ask and I tell all and all and all. Now what Lord? Now I know that not everyone tells all or lays their cards on the table. My mistake was in thinking everyone was honest and open. Do I play games?

Shut up! Shut up! Don't tell all. Again I feel the loneliness coming in. Never has my husband answered one question without asking one first. To shut up is to be lonely. To step out of the lives and let them come to me.

Oh Lord You are asking another biggy. To step out of the picture and not be so available. To step out and not let them know where I am at. To let them find me. Oh Lord Jesus, You were like that. You waited until they asked, until they were ready.

Teach me to shut up. Teach me to sit back and watch. Teach me to not play games nor get hooked into playing their games with them.

Give me the strength to be alone. Loneliness is so frightening

My Window Prayer

to me. I know You will be with me. Teach me to rely on Your presence.

Lord Jesus, You truly are strong!

How do I describe not being able to discern the things that are right in front of you? How do I describe the way a person can be so manipulated and still claim intelligence? How can we be so naïve? I did not have the skills to be a judge of what was going on in front of me.

To give you an idea of what it is like. On my 18th birthday my mother gave me a scholarship to a beauty school. I was not asked if I wanted to be a beauty operator, but I went anyway because I had this present. I never did like it and didn't want it. When you have been told how to think you don't think for yourself. Again that is the result of not having the self worth. I sometimes think that I floated through life with no direction.

Keeping my life in my control has been a lifetime of work. I am still working on it. There are many ways that a person can be manipulated. One of the ways is not being paid attention to, being put down, being beat down, and so many other ways. It takes the grace of God to dig these out and even than it is hard to undo a lifetime to over come being a victim..

I think we all have a tendency to control our life and

the lives around us. Controlling someone is not love. There is a fine line between controlling and helping. Even with the best intentions, you can use too much control and wipe someone out.

These games that are played with people can be unintentional or they can be just a game. Selfishness is so damaging. Do we have a right to want others to do our will?

The way we control the things and people around us comes in many degrees. Some of us are not aware of how we do this and others are always planning to get what we want. How do we protect ourselves? I have learned that I don't think like a manipulator and therefore do not recognize it when it comes at me. The games that are played can be for fun. Teasing and bullying can be some of these things. Other things can be as a possessive thing or a way of isolating a person from others. How can you see this or what can be done?

I have only recognized this through prayer. It can be so suttle that it is hard to know that you are not making your own decisions. If you are a victim of this it can be a habit hard to break. It can also be hard to give up the game playing if you are the one playing the game. It is important to know both sides of this. Knowing this can help both to have a better relationship. Of course this takes work for both, but willingness is again a must.

If you are not a decision maker you leave your self open

My Window Prayer

for someone to control you. Learn to make your mind up in the little things and than move to more important things. If you don't handle your own life than there always seem to be someone that will handle for you. It doesn't matter if they appear kind and doing this for your own good, they are doing it. No, you are letting them do it. Try to keep your life in your control and give when you need.

Conversation

What is conversation? How do we have two-way communication?

My conversations have mostly been about myself. Just ask me and you can have my life story. Just ask and you can have my life. Just ask and you will not exist. I can wipe a person out.

I need to have people around me. Is that insecurity? Oh Lord, how long I have wanted to be liked. No to be loved. That was so hard for me to say. I don't even have a life I am so dependent on others. The way they treat me. The way they talk to me. My existence depends on how I am treated.

"People pay me lip service but their heart is far from me," this is out of the Bible. This is one side of the story. "It is not what

goes into a man's mouth that makes him impure, it is what comes out of his mouth." Oh Lord I am guilty of both. I am negative and selfish. I have not loved the other person nor have I said good things about my neighbor.

Oh Lord I can see how I have been so unchristian in my conversation.

"What comes out of the mouth originates in the mind." Teach me how to think with You. Teach me how to talk to others. I once was a happy person to be with, making fun of myself putting myself down. Teach me to laugh at myself but not negatively. Help me to like myself and not be so dependent on the people around me. Help me to be OK with just me.

Lord Jesus, You are my strength, my friend.

When you look to others, as I have, to give you that first value of love, you won't find it. So my need for this value had to be healed. One of the most valuable things in conversation is listening. Not think of what you are going to say. Listening with both ears.

Listening also requires a nonjudgmental attitude, should I say an expectance of the person. Giving value to that person. Not to wipe the person out. How did I get my conversation under control? I am not sure that I have. It is an ongoing process. I am better than I was. Leaving things unsaid because it isn't necessary to say everything that comes to mind is what I have been working on.

Patience is also a requirement. It does take some people longer to express themselves. Can I keep quiet long enough to hear what is the point. Well, I am trying. Nothing I have to say is worth any more than what others are saying to me.

Asking the right questions without going to far into personal things is also a lesson. That is none of my business is a good thing to say if I ask too much. The way I handle it if I am asked too much is to say I don't care to answer that. I have been known to say I don't feel that is for me to say. Keeping control of the conversation is also an art.

Repeating things that are said to me is another requirement. Weather someone says it is a secret or not does matter. If the third party wants people to know they will express it to others. This is especially important if the conversation is personal. I have painful memories of not following this rule of thumb.

You've heard that you don't talk politics or religion, well there is some truth to that. Know the person you are talking to. Some subjects are better than others are. These are not the only subjects that are to be bypassed.

What you think is what you are, so that comes out in your conversation. I keep trying to think the best of others. Some times I can do better than other times. How you say something is more important than what you have to say. Chose your words carefully. I keep trying to think before I open my mouth. That takes practice and I am practicing. I find that if I think well of others and things I make less mistakes and have to eat my words. Most of the time I can apologize and go on. Some times I have to seek the person out and rectify the situation. Once in awhile my foot finds my mouth.

Being able to go back and change the mistakes helps make me humble, but the feeling of being free of guilt is worth it. Communication is really an art. Sometimes there are misunderstanding of where someone is coming from and there is a feeling that can come before reason. Always take a second to stop the anger or hurt from color your reason. This I know is easier said than done.

Motherhood

8

Oh Lord, how easy it was to conceive them! Now what? How do I become a mother?

How do I let go? How do I stand back and watch? How do I teach? How do I love?

The bible says, "Do not anger your children. Bring them up with the training and instruction befitting the Lord." What if they aren't listening? It also says, " Do not nag your children least they lose heart," For the fourth time hang up your jacket.

The art of listening and asking questions. That's what it is all about. Find out where they are coming from. Find out from them how they are feeling or thinking. Don't assume you know until it is proven. Set the rules, follow through, and let God do the rest.

When they fall and they are human, be there. Then is when love is most needed. Love them rain or shine.

My pride is in the way. I have too much pride in them.

Their life is not your life. They are not a part of you. You can't possess them. They are not to love your desires through but their own.

Teach them the way of the Lord and then let them find Him. Jesus is with them. Jesus is the way.

Lord Jesus, once again I ask for strength to do what I can and let the rest in Your hands. To teach, to discipline, and to do it with love.

Lord Jesus make me a mother.

One of the things that was a blessing to me is the order in my home that came with my window prayer. The discipline in our house started with me. A needed to learn how to handle things and take time to do this. I had to learn to put the children first and be consistent in my handling of the consequences. God gave me this task first. To take charge and do what I could to organize and teach.

Having a work chart for the kids was one thing I have to do. Teaching the kids that they to needed to be

My Window Prayer

responsible for the care of the home. The work was rotated for each week. No one was given a greater job for more than a week. My youngest son was help on occasion because of his age. With this the kids were given an idea that Dad worked hard for the things we had and we needed to take care of them.

To teach them to save and about money they were saving aluminum and putting away money for a bike. The money was in a saving account and I let them know how much they had. Some chose to add to it with money they received for presents. How proud they were with their new bikes. The boy across the street got a new bike and they asked him how much he paid for it. The reply was that he saved 13 dollars from work he did and his dad paid the rest. What a difference, the bikes in our house were worth over 100 dollars and all earned. The kids knew the difference in working for things and not getting things handed to them.

When there were jackets laying all over in the entryway, they disappeared. The next morning as they were to go to school, they asked for their coats. My reply was I don't know did you hang them up. What are we to wear? Maybe your snowmobile suits. It didn't take long for the jackets to be hung up. Same for the toys, when they were on the floor at the end of the day they disappeared. Where are they, did you put them away. When they reappeared later it was like Christmas all over again, and the toys were finding their way back to the toy box.

Tough love is part of loving. The punishment should be a teaching tool to make restitution as often as possible. It was sometimes an embarrassment to me, as having to march the kid back to the store with something taken. Some times my punishment didn't fit the crime and I am sorry for that. One of the Bill Cosby jokes is that it isn't fare that a parent has one child so they always know who did it. Sometimes you can get the wrong kid. I learn to get the right one or not to issue consequences.

Checking on the homes that they were going to, having a set time for homework and making it a quiet time, and other things that I had been given to do. This all took work and diligence and I was learning to be consistent in all things. God was good to me to teach me much about what needed to be done.

I see many more things that I could have done in hindsight, but I did a best I could. Do I regret some things, yes. Do I feel it is to late, no. I try every time I see them to let them know I care. I will probably always fall short, but I will keep trying.

Children also learn from what they see. Do they see love between the parents or do they see disharmony? Do they hear please and thank you or do they see no appreciation? Do they see good living or do they

My Window Prayer

see immorality? Do they see negativity and a positive attitude? They are like little receivers gathering what they see and hear.

The responsibility of raising the children can be heavy or thought of as a blessing. I can tell you that those years go faster than you think. The chose to give in love is worth it.

Living With A Nonchristian 9

Confusion! Confusion! Confusion! Lord what am I to do? How do I read You? What are You saying to me?

Self pity is so loud I can't hear You. The bitterness is so strong I can't see what it is I'm to do. Oh Lord the ache in my body for Your touch, Your wisdom, Your strength, and YOUR patience. Patience, PATIENCE, that word is so hard.

Lord the unbeliever I live worth is bringing an evil force into my house. The Bible says" If any woman has a husband who is an unbeliever but is willing to live with her, she must not divorce him. The unbeliever is consecrated by his believing wife.

If it were otherwise, your children should be unclean; but as it is, they are holy."

Oh God, is that true? Of course everything in the Bible is true! Oh Lord that means You are protecting my kids. Praise God! But what about my bitterness. That is selfishness? Yes I'm hurt because he does not love me the way I know a husband should. The way I hear about in a believer. Oh Lord we are right back to expectations. There is still so much of the old man alive that I am hurt, rejected, alone, and longing for something better. Is that it, the old man is alive.

Kay says to teach him. He is so unwilling a student. Tough love. Oh Lord, tough love. Meet number one coward, me. Tough love. Stand firm against the evil but not against the person. With out teaching him it is like cutting off his head despite his face. But he doesn't want to hear. It doesn't matter what he wants. He can leave.

Once again I come to complete surrender into Your hands. I don't want to face divorce and all that goes with it. Once again I must trust You. Have faith and hope and trust.

Dear Lord give me strength and willingness to do Your will.

How does one judge the spirituality of another person? By the way they act or by their fruit. The physical hurt of pain is easy to see. The emotional pain is something else.

Christians that are growing in the spirit can still have moments of unloving, but they should be learning by

My Window Prayer

their mistakes and always trying to do better. The only way I am aware of my shortcomings is the conscience that God gives me. When we want the best for someone else that is love. When we pit ourselves against the very person we are to love, that is not love.

When we are not adding to the health of the home, we are not thinking the best for those in it. Always seeing the glass half empty and not giving the praise and good will of the people in our home is destructive. Bringing a negative spirit in a home brings disharmony and upheaval to everything in that home.

The loving spirit helps the children in that home to grow and make good decisions. They grow emotionally and reach the age of reason. When we give in time and effort to the home it tends to show. That is good time and effort. God can bring a loving spirit in a home if the parents are willing to give their lives to Him.

If you are in an unchristian relationship and thinking about marriage be very careful. The things that you think will change may not. There are many things in your future that can come back to this day.

When we are on the same page with all things it becomes easier. Of course some things change in the middle years and that does give us the need for prayer and commitment. If you are a Christian, being married to a Christian gives you a special bond and communication.

Your life style can change with the influence of the other. Sometimes that is not a good change.

Is it important to be as much on the same page is possible? If you want to live in peace and harmony, you bet. Taking a class before marriage can be an eye opener. They cover many things that you need to talk about before marriage. It's a big step, take it seriously. In this day of easy divorce it may seem that it is nothing, but it is a comment to love each other. There are many things that come up that you may not be aware of and it is not easy. Make good decisions. Pray for them and give them up to God. Getting out of the way is hard.

That is the last of my laments. I write this for my children to give them an idea of my path through life. Did God make good on the prayers at the end of the laments? Well, he has and it is on going. The work is never done. I am better than I was and hope to be better in the future. This has been about forty-year journey and I will always be learning.

There have been highs and lows and some very hard things. It is good to remember that the sun always comes out after a storm. The Son is there through the storm. The labor here on earth will prepare us for the glories of heaven. The one thing that God will ask you on that day of judgement is," how did you love the ones I put in your every day to love." Many of the people we meet in a day are just there for than and now, like a clerk in a store. We can be inpatient and take that out on the clerk. We can remember there is more at stake than today.

The way to happiness can be a surprise if you try to be content with what you have today. If we slow down to COUNT OUR BLESSINGS we can be happy. If we have food on our plates and a roof over our heads, we are blessed. Look to the positives and not what you do have. If we show our gratitude we can make ourselves more satisfied with life.

There is more danger in this world than you are aware of. The desensitizing of our morals, the occult, the negative message in music, and many more things than have become the norm. When I look back, I see that most people were on the same page. The schools were teaching the 3 rs and not the social things that are the parents duty. The TV was fun not vulgar. The church was giving the same message. This has been a slippery slide into a world that has been much more lost. Are you happy? Are you satisfied with your life? Are you looking for something?

Healing from the past was all wrapped up in the work of coming to know and love God. Many times it was in the hard times that I grew the most. I come to know the sun did shine and was brighter than before when I went through those times. It is not for the faint of heart. But it takes that heart felt prayer to invite God into your life. As my window prayer was a desperate cry for help, you can also reap the rewards. I pray that this book can bring you an understanding of my walk with God and the way of love.

When my family gets together it is so wonderful to hear them enjoy each other. It is the reward of the hard work. This world holds a lot of danger for my grandchildren. I can only trust in God's never ending love for me and mine. GOD BLESS ALL OF YOU AMEN!!!

CPSIA information can be obtained at www.ICGtesting.com
Printed in the USA
BVOW081553170413

318426BV00001B/23/P